For my mother and father

About the Author

JIM NOLAN grew up in Buffalo, New York, where 20 of his Listener Commentaries have aired on WBFO 88.7 Public Radio. His writing has appeared in *The New Yorker, McSweeney's Internet Tendency, Maisonneuve,* and *Family Fun.*

Jim lives downstate with his wife and two sons. To read or hear more, go to **jimnolansblog.com** or **youtube.com/jimnolan3**.

Table of Contents

A French Poodle in Buffalo	01
Niagara River Death Cruise	05
The Red Barn Incident	07
Ghosts of Halloweens Past	11
The Secret of Math	13
The Incredible, Inedible Egg	15
To the Class of '10, From the Class of '12	19
The *Real* Most Dangerous Game	21
The Right to Bear Beef-on-Weck	23
1970s Teenage Human Shield	27
Your Windsong Stays on (What's Left of) My Mind	29
Forged in Buffalo	33
World Gone *MAD*	35
Night of the Grizzly	39
Welcome, Canadian Overlords	42

Preface

I AM NOT LUCKY enough to live in Buffalo anymore; work has taken me elsewhere. But I live there psychologically to an extent that concerns my wife, even though she is also a displaced Buffalonian and should understand. Perhaps it's her unease with my scarfing down wings like they were M&Ms. She thinks they're unhealthy—forgetting that, like a car's engine, your heart needs lubrication.

Buffalo has a tired reputation as a depressed Rust Belt city, but that's just a front the Chamber of Commerce puts out to keep others away. The city is in many ways a paradise, and they don't want it ruined. For one thing, Buffalo has such plentiful water that residents bathe every day there, a habit soon to disappear in the South and West. They live beside a now-pristine Lake Erie, and you're not getting any of it—they just passed a law. All you people who moved away to warmer, more arid climes: you'll just have to move back.

Besides, you never should have left in the first place. When Buffalonian Willis Carrier invented air conditioning, he did so for industrial uses, never imaging it would suck the city's population away to previously uninhabitable places like Atlanta or Houston or Phoenix. Carrier now rests uneasily in Buffalo's Forest Lawn, eternally regretting this turn of fate.

The good news is when you do move back, you'll find 125-year-old handcrafted five-bedroom homes on broad, leafy avenues for sale for $12.99, just slightly more than the beef-on-weck sandwiches found only here. The Buffalo wings (which they simply call "wings," like the French call French fries *frites*) are only tasty in the Queen City. I'm sorry, but this is true. Outside of Buffalo the technology simply doesn't exist, and this time they're keeping the patents to themselves. They're not making the same mistake they made with air conditioning.

When Samuel Johnson famously thundered, "When a man is tired of Buffalo, he is tired of life,"[1] he was right, as usual. I would move back in a second if I could, and one day I will. Until then, I'll just have to write about how wonderful it was to grow up there, contentedly ensconced among the only people in America with the sense to understand the importance of a loganberry to a char-broiled hot.

Hastings-on-Hudson, NY
June 2011

P.S. Many of these stories first appeared as Listener Commentaries on the State University of New York at Buffalo's public radio station, WBFO 88.7. I am grateful to it.

---

[1] *The Journal of a Tour to the Hebrides and Western New York with Samuel Johnson, LL.D.* James Boswell, 1786. "Dr. Johnson had for many years given me hopes that we should go together, and visit Buffalo."

A French Poodle in Buffalo

YOU KNOW HOW DOGS resemble their owners? Well, they also take on the characteristics of the families they join. So the dogs my family had when I was growing up in Snyder were a little, well, eccentric. Especially Oscar. Oscar was named after a cat—which probably didn't help his reputation among the neighborhood dogs, paticularly since he was a smallish French poodle.

Oscar came from pedigree stock, sired of a champion, we children were told. His full name, befitting such august lineage, was Sir Oscar of Burbank, the name of the street on which we lived. Pretty fancy moniker for a dog that looked forward to garbage day as if he had booked a favored table at the Park Lane.

We lavished upon Oscar all the love we were less comfortable expressing to one another. This made it all the more peculiar that he acted like we were trying to poison him at mealtime. We'd set down his bowl of dog chow and he'd sniff it for a minute or two before taking a small, precautionary nibble. If that didn't kill him, he'd eat a little more, uneasily.

Maybe he was remembering the Nembutal pill we'd slip him when we took him in the car on our way to Cape Cod. Nembutal, a powerful barbiturate, caused him to walk sideways, a novel and entertaining sight at rest stops along the New York State Thruway. For some families, it might have been the highlight of their vacations.

Being French, Oscar was of a romantic nature, but his forays into continuing his line were, to our knowledge, unsuccessful. He used to disappear for hours on end, until we'd get a call from someone asking us to come and stop him from barking on their lawn. They'd invariably add that Oscar was late, that their dog was no longer in heat, and that all the other suitors had been by a week or two earlier. Looking back on it, I see that in the vacuum of any advice from my father I may have unconsciously adopted Oscar's dating tactics in my teenage years, with the same measure of success.

Oscar had no more luck chasing squirrels. He would bark endlessly at them in the trees, urging them to come down and let his powerful poodle jaws end their useless, furry lives. They would just laugh at him in squirrel—which he understood—only further enraging his proud Gallic nature.

Oscar lived a long time: 98 dog years. Toward the end, he had to get up in the middle of the night to relieve himself. Rather than inconvenience us, he simply used the Persian rug in the study. We never knew this until one December night, when Mom had a sleepover guest and pulled out the folding couch for her in that room, thoughtfully turning up the thermostat to make her comfortable. Over the course of the evening the carpet marinated, causing the study to smell like the men's room at War Memorial Stadium during the late fourth quarter of a Bills game. I don't think their friendship survived the incident.

Oscar's passing hit us hard, but not so hard that I couldn't suggest we stuff him and place him forever on the feather settee he slept on all those years. I was overruled. My family has since admitted that maybe it wasn't such a crazy idea. Twenty-five years later, we still miss the old gent so much. But we are not without our memories. Especially when we spend any time in the study.

Mother never could bear to throw away that rug.

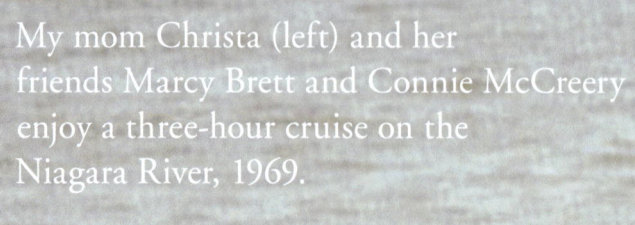

My mom Christa (left) and her friends Marcy Brett and Connie McCreery enjoy a three-hour cruise on the Niagara River, 1969.

Groovy pants, Mom.

Niagara River Death Cruise

AT FIRST GLANCE, my father has little in common with Gilligan of "Gilligan's Island." But the resemblance became all too clear to an unlucky group of partiers who were invited to celebrate his 40th birthday on a 38-foot cabin cruiser on the Niagara River. It was 1969, and it was meant to be a three-hour tour.

Many of the details of this historic voyage are, for reasons you'll discover, at best hazily recollected by my father. So I decided to interview actual witnesses to his legendary lapse of judgment that left the boat completely disabled and headed towards the deadly 170-foot drop of Niagara Falls.

The trip started out with little indication of the coming debacle. The owner of the boat, life-long West Ferry Street resident Tim Urban, felt comfortable allowing my father, an old Navy hand, to skipper the boat. The six couples riding along likewise trusted that my father's place at the helm posed little risk to them or the future security of the 14 children they had collectively left at home.

For a while, they were right. They left Jafco Marina and circled Grand Island, consuming the chicken salad sandwiches my mother made and, as Tim puts it, "adult beverages." On the way back to Jafco, my father decided they should tootle up to the Lake, passing under the Peace Bridge along the way.

It was then that Tim decided to tell my father that he was under no circumstances to pull a particular switch on the console. The wisdom of telling this to Dad can, with the luxury of hindsight, be called into question. Because my father immediately pulled said switch, instantly rendering the boat powerless.

Pulled by the 13-knot current of Lake Erie emptying into the river, the boat reversed course, heading inexorably towards the immense steel-plated supports of the Peace Bridge.

It would take a psychologist greater than Dr. Phil to understand my father's motivation for pulling the forbidden switch. I suspect the real reason was that he was seized by what Poe called "the imp of the perverse," a creature that makes you take nonsensical, self-destructive actions.

Genny Cream Ales offer a less literary explanation.

The radio having no power, Tim fired off distress flares just before the Chris Craft shot past the bridge supports, coming within five feet of being torn into splinters. Tim tells me that cars in Fort Erie honked at them in appreciation for the show they were putting on.

After also narrowly missing the Massachusetts Intake and the International Railroad Bridge, Tim decided to drop anchor. It finally took hold in the middle of the river not far from Jafco. They weren't going to go over the Falls; their children would not be orphaned. Soon the Coast Guard came and towed them back to the marina.

I recently tried to organize a 40th anniversary party in celebration of the ill-fated voyage, retracing the route on a rented cabin cruiser with Tim and my father at the helm.

As it turned out, everybody was busy that weekend.

The Red Barn Incident

EVERY FAMILY HAS legendary episodes that are known only to them. They are often identified by a catch phrase that sounds innocuous enough to outsiders but is rich in meaning to Mom, Dad and the kids. In my family, it's the Red Barn Incident.

Some of you might remember the Red Barn—a fast-food outlet that served fried chicken and was cleverly shaped like… a red barn. We used to frequent the one on Kensington Avenue near Harlem Road in the early '70s. It was to be the unlikely stage for my father's role as Ozzie Nelson gone Ozzy Osbourne.

It started innocently enough—Dad venturing out in his navy blue '68 Mustang to get some chicken for the family, bringing my brother Chris along to run in and fetch a bucket. Chris, 11 at the time, placed the order. And waited. And waited. And waited. How long is a matter of some dispute. Chris says 10 minutes; my father, 35. Finally Dad could take it no longer. He strode into the store and began to yell at the poor people behind the counter, to my brother's utter mortification. Now, I've only heard my father lose his temper twice—excluding the golf course, where he expresses himself with a limited and atypical vocabulary almost every time he hits the ball. Dad's exact quote, according to Chris, was "that's an awful long time to keep a kid waiting," showing an uncharacteristic concern for Chris's busy schedule watching "Commander Tom" and reading *MAD* Magazine. Soon the chicken came, gingerly handed over, I suppose, by some terrified counter person, and Dad and Chris left, never to return.

Red Barn closed that location soon after. It was inevitable, really, after they caused my mild-mannered father to lose his temper so far from the putting green.

To any of you who may have been working at Red Barn that day: I'm sure my father regrets the incident, deep, deep down. And to everyone making wings at Duff's or La Nova: Please don't keep my dad waiting. You don't want him "going Red Barn" on you.

The plastic masks were already beginning to suffocate us. We didn't care.

Ghosts of Halloweens Past

FOR HALLOWEEN ONE YEAR, my son Edward was an M&M, an unpaid walking billboard for the billion-dollar, privately held Mars Candy Corporation.

Fair enough, he loves M&Ms. Although I still hold out hope he'll one day be a Kit Kat man like his father or any other right-thinking adult.

One year, Eddie chose to recycle his green sequined frog costume. It became a galaxy, a spangly green galaxy (we'd been taking him to the planetarium a lot). When he turned around in it, he looked like an elongated disco ball.

When I was young, my own choice in costuming was somewhat less complex, and not informed by astronomy. Most years I went as a pirate, because it involved rubbing a burnt cork all over my face. Elvis never had fuller sideburns than I did those years.

Alternatively, I would buy a flimsy plastic mask and whatever flammable polyester outfit that came with it. I believe I was Johnny Quest one year, and I seem to recall a Deputy Dog get-up.

While these ensembles were convenient, the masks had the unfortunate drawback of becoming moist, cold and clammy as you tried to breathe out of their tiny plastic mouths. Your friends couldn't understand a single word you said, which was fine: you weren't there to socialize, you were there to get as much candy as humanly possible. What little conversation there was centered on the appropriateness of doubling back to those houses with the best sweets.

It wasn't surprising that Eddie would create a unique costume, or at least repackage his old one in such a completely different way. His great love back then, besides his mother and Pikachu, was inventing.

Edward invented enough gizmos to keep the U.S. Patent Office busy for years—although truthfully, not all of them had a practical side. In fact, I'm not sure one comes to mind that had commercial applications. A cardboard sink. A house for a mouse complete with pool and attached garage. Recipes for "forest salad" and "blue cake"... these are not items consumers are clamoring for.

His mother's creative streak is equally impressive, explaining the Bee Gees-style frog costume she fashioned for him all those Halloweens ago. In Eddie's mind, each reflective sequin of her handiwork was a star. Collectively, they became an interstellar mass of intensity and brightness unsurpassed by a baker's dozen supernovas. If you held the flashlight right.

Nowadays Eddie doesn't go trick-or-treating. He's too old. His brother George still goes, though. George seems to favor a pirate costume. I'm waiting for the Human Genome Project to identify the gene.

The Secret of Math

THERE COMES A TIME in every child's life when he realizes his parent isn't perfect. This was mine.

When I was in second grade, Dad promised to tell me, and I quote, "the secret of math." I eagerly awaited this closely guarded information that adults were surely forbidden to tell their kids. Dad was going to break every rule in the grown-up canon! And then he told me the secret in, I believe, a whisper. "A sharp pencil, Jimmie. A sharp pencil."

Another reason for therapy: I was raised to believe that Dad's childhood dog, Smokey, could talk. He told me that Smokey was capable of enunciating "I want one!" with all the clarity of James Earl Jones. This led to my raising my hand in second grade to set Mrs. Hermann straight about her notion that animals were inarticulate. I can still hear the class's laughter ringing in my ears.[2]

Almost as traumatic, Dad had a cavalier attitude towards Santa Claus. One Christmas morning—as a matter of fact, not long after the sharp pencil incident—Dad told me that just before he nodded off he heard the sound of hooves on our snowy roof. Not only did he not arise from his winter's nap and throw up the sash, he didn't wake me, either.

Dad has many good points, but he's no Clement C. Moore.

At times Dad lived life dangerously. I need only bring up the incident when he used his knees to steer the car so his hands were free to unwrap a piece of gum. After having witnessed this behavior, I never again wondered why Dad, a doctor, was not allowed to drive an ambulance. Probably he unwrapped a piece of gum like that in front of his boss. Smaller slips have ruined careers.

Now that I'm 43, I suppose I should forgive him and move on. And I will, right after I buy my nine-year-old son a pencil sharpener.

---

[2] Of course, now it turns out dogs *can* talk. There's a Siberian husky named Mishka on YouTube that can say "I love you." This has shaken me to my core—Dad was telling the truth. I think.

The Incredible, Inedible Egg

IT'S NOT EASY getting two boys out of bed for school. Sometimes I have to physically lift them and place their feet on the floor with a lively encouragement that my wife calls "yelling."

This is essentially my father's revenge on me for similar, if not worse, behavior. But at least *my* boys don't have to look forward to the breakfast my dad had waiting for me, which was enough to make any 12-year-old pull the covers over his head.

Dad used to scramble eggs and then put them on a hot plate to await what I suppose he hoped would be us eagerly tucking into them. But by the time I got downstairs the hot plate had not only kept the eggs warm, it had reduced them to a hot, rubbery mass. Really hot.

Now, my father wasn't, and isn't, what you'd call a cook (outside of an acknowledged barbeque prowess). But the poor man took pride in his terrible eggs and couldn't understand why we ate the lumpy mass so slowly. In part, we were trying not to burn the roofs of our mouths.

Some might point out that if I got out of bed when my father first awakened me the eggs would have been fine, maybe even fluffy and delicious. In fact, Dad did point this out. So did Mom, when she came downstairs.

Dad used to give Mom a new robe every Christmas, and she would wear it on winter mornings. Frankly, they weren't the most stylish or attractive robes in the world—my dad picked them out and it was the '70s, a combination that might be considered the perfect storm of fashion disaster—but they *were* functional. They reached right down to the floor, and could be used to sweep it if you wanted.

Maybe these annual warm robes were my dad's way of saying he was sorry for moving to Buffalo from Honolulu, where they began their marriage in 1956 when he was in the Navy. It was, I think, a classic bait-and-switch. I can only imagine the incredulous look on my poor mother's face as she opened yet another robe on Christmas morning: "Gee, this one's a lovely burnt orange. Thanks dear."

Dad might have been inspired by the color of our shag carpeting that year. I guess you could say that in her own unique, unfortunately colored way, Mom suffered in the mornings just like us kids. At the hands of my well-meaning father.

Our poodle suffered as well. Dad would let Oscar outside and Oscar would return so completely covered with little balls of snow attached to his fur that they would weigh his little body down and he'd collapse onto the linoleum floor until they melted.

Once I tried to slip him some of Dad's scrambled eggs as he lay there. Oscar wouldn't have anything to do with them, either.

The Buffalo Central High Class of 1912.
My grandfather, the Class Poet, stands in
the top row, sixth from the right.

To the Class of '10,
From the Class of '12

TO THE CLASS OF 2010:

I speak to you today across a chasm of incomprehension. You are teenagers. I was once like you, but now that experience is lost to me, as the ring of Santa's sleigh bell is to grown-ups in *The Polar Express*. To recall what it was like even fleetingly, I have to watch a John Hughes film.

So instead of forcing you to listen to the watch-outs and naggings of one of my decrepitude, I offer you the hope and optimism of another graduating class, the Buffalo Central High School Class of '12. 1912. My grandfather graduated with it. I have their commencement booklet, *The Calendar*. It, unlike them, is in mint condition.

The Calendar includes a Class Prophecy, in which every student's future is revealed by looking through a "small, beautifully colored piece of glass" given to the author by a "dainty fairy." Alas, the glass must have been somehow cracked, for here is what is prophesized for my grandfather:

"But by far the wealthiest of the class shall be J. Paul Nolan, whose practical common sense will make him successful in Wall Street." I guess practical common sense was as little valued by Wall Street back then as it is now, or J. Paul simply had the sense not to go there. He stayed in Buffalo and worked as a purchasing agent for Pratt & Lambert.

The prophet continues:

"Jacob Sicherman will be a prominent business and literary man in a western city."

Actually, Jake became a Buffalo lawyer. His daughter Barbara would become a groundbreaking historian of the women's movement, and the women of the Class of 1912 were determined to give her something to write about. Many of the class officers and academic prize-winners were women, seven years before women could vote.

Here's what the prophet foresees for three of them: "The Mayor of Cleveland, the Honorable Helen Abrams, Chief of the Fire Dept., Evadne Hea, and the noted Architect Bessie Rosenthal showed me plainly what women were to do in a short time."

What advice would the Class of 1912 give to you? Hard to say. There's not a lot of it in *The Calendar,* other than that old standby to be true to your school. Maybe they just weren't into advice as much as we are today. Maybe they understood the futility of it, and had a better grasp of the capriciousness of life. They went on to face a depression sandwiched by two world wars, the Bomb, assassinations and Howard Cosell.

No, the only advice I can find in the entire booklet comes from the Class Poem. I close with a stanza from it, written 98 short years ago by my grandfather and namesake. It not only offers better counsel than I can—it rhymes. Kind of.

> *So let no cloud obscure the summer sky,*
> *Enjoy June's beauty while the heart is young.*
> *The Past is bright, but buoyant youth replies:*
> *The Past is nothing, life has scarce begun.*

The *Real* Most Dangerous Game

I COULD MAKE a bunch of recommendations to politicians facing elections. But for male voters like me, one issue rises above the rest.

Jarts.

It's high time this country brought them back, and stopped it with the namby-pambiness. The nanny-state nonsense.

Jarts were weighted lawn darts that you'd toss thirty or so yards into a circular target, and just because they were basically lethal, sharpened steel projectiles, the Consumer Products Safety Commission saw fit to ban 'em in 1988. C'mon, that's crazy. What's next, seat belt laws?

We used to play Jarts out at a friend's farm and nobody got killed, although our Springer Spaniel Hannah did get hit once, on the butt. It bounced off her considerable girth like a superball.

It's hard to remember the grown-ups playing the game without a cocktail in hand, which probably did not help their accuracy any. As the day wore on, the graceful arc of the missile became more and more erratic, and the circumference of the Jart's landing area expanded ever outward. I seem to recall a Jart or two ending up in the branches of the apple tree. They're probably still up there.

I wonder what would happen if you got caught with a set today. The police would probably book you and take you on a perp walk; you'd be all over Eyewitness News and TMZ. There are probably guys who meet secretly, late at night, in Delaware Park when the moon is low and play, with sentries posted so they can scram if need be. Their wives have no idea, because no woman would ever condone the game's deadly beauty, putting first—as women so often do—her toddler's survival.

I don't care if they lock me up. I'm buying a set on eBay. No jury of my male peers would ever convict me. So heads up kids, dogs, cats and apple tree squirrels. Daddy needs to relax with a couple of beers and his Jarts. Oops, look out, look out!

The Right to Bear Beef-on-Weck

PROPONENTS OF the second amendment claim we'll only take their guns by prying them from their cold, dead hands. Well, I have some items you'll have to pry from my lifeless fingers too, although none as yet enjoy constitutional protection.

One. My *Lord of the Rings* extended version movie collection. I've watched *LOTR* so many times even my sons have tired of it, and my wife has threatened to go on a long vacation with an uncertain return date. I think my ever-more-frequent quoting of the characters—"Muster the Rohirrim!"—is finally proving too much for her.

Two. My digital recording of "West End Girls" by the Pet Shop Boys. Four minutes and 46 seconds of pure mopey, synthpop deliciousness. When I hear it I am 24 again.

Three. *The Code of the Woosters*, by P.G. Wodehouse. The greatest work of art in the English language and, coincidentally, the funniest. In fact, every single word in it is funny. Including the prepositions.

Four. The eight-millimeter footage my dad shot on a hand-cranked Kodak movie camera back in the '60s. Dad was an *auteur* of the backyard birthday party. Ingmar Bergman was obsessed with death; my father was obsessed with Vin-Chet cakes.

Five and six. A Ted's hot dog and an Anderson's custard. Wanna bite? Get your own.

Seven. My collection of *MAD* Magazines from the early '70s, back when they were "35 cents cheap." I met Al Jaffe at a cartoonists' party in December of 2010. I embarrassed myself by fawning all over him. I mean, it was *Al Jaffe*. What else was I supposed to do? Okay, maybe I didn't need to actually genuflect.

Eight. My CDs of Jim Dale reading the seven Harry Potter books. The fifth book alone is 27 hours long. We listened to it in its entirety on a family vacation to Nova Scotia. The boys and I were enthralled; my wife began to develop a nasty twitch as I put in CD #19.

The Founding Fathers were wise enough to allow the Constitution to change with the times, and Americans have done well by it except for the Prohibition mistake, which Buffalonians of the time considered more of a suggestion than a law. Still, I will not push for a 28th Amendment protecting my right to beef-on-weck. That right does not yet seem under threat. And the federal government has no room on its plate for delectable Buffalo food right now.

Replace Oscar with Cujo and you have the approximate staging of what was to occur ten years later.

1970s Teenage Human Shield

THIS IS THE STORY my father has begged me not to write. But I will, if only to bring comfort to other children whose parents have willfully placed them in mortal danger.

It started innocently enough. My father and I out for a jog, a couple times around the block on a cold November night in 1975.

Suddenly, a gigantic dog, barking madly, ran towards us with the velocity of a runaway train. My father did what any loving parent would have done: he placed me between himself and Cujo, like a human shield. The dog was so surprised by this dereliction of parental duty that he stopped, shook his head in disbelief, and turned away.

It made the rest of the decade a little awkward between me and Dad.

Over the years, he has offered various explanations for his behavior. I've always liked this one: it broke his heart to do it, but as the primary breadwinner, he had to think of the rest of the family. He also claimed biblical precedence, citing Abraham's sacrifice of Isaac. But as I pointed out, Dad was not under orders from God (unless he was hearing voices again).

In his defense, this was not Dad's first run-in with the beast. He had been menaced by the hellhound several times before. I think Dad believed that it had a specific animus towards him alone, and he acted accordingly. Perhaps he was right. The dog didn't attack *me*.

Still, I mentioned to Dad that on Mutual of Omaha's *Wild Kingdom*, Marlon Perkins often pointed out the mommy or daddy animal's fierce instinct to protect its young. Hang on... come to think of it... it's always the *mother* animal doing the fighting. In nature, the dad's role in raising the young is pretty much nonexistent. And believe me, my mother would have sent that dog packing. So from a biological standpoint, I was running with the wrong parent.

Now that I have my own 16-year-old boy, I understand my father's actions better, and my son is way better behaved than I ever was. Knowing what Dad was putting up with, it's only surprising that he didn't wrap me in bacon and knock me over the head with a stick as the dog approached.

So Dad, all is forgiven. I'll go running with you anytime.

As long as Mom comes along.

Your Windsong Stays on (What's Left of) My Mind

"I CAN'T SEEM to forget you. Your Windsong stays on my, Windsong stays on my, Windsong stays on my mind."

I'd do anything to drive that jingle from my mind. Now that I'm 50, and forgetting words like "house," my brain doesn't have room for 1970s relics. Here are some other things that have stayed on my mind since my first, unfortunate encounter with them.

"Simple Simon Says" by the 1910 Fruitgum Company. They also tortured us with "1-2-3 Red Light" and "Indian Giver," a song that not only insults Native Americans but one's cerebral cortex as well. Simple Simon says get electroshock therapy to wipe these tunes from memory. I wonder if my health plan covers that.

For some reason I frequently recall a commercial with a famous fashion designer in it. He begins the spot by saying, "My name"—dramatic pause—"is Emilio Pucci." I can't seem to forget that ad, either. Emilio Pucci stays on my mind.

The shampoo "Gee, Your Hair Smells Terrific." No man in recorded history, or even pre-history, had ever uttered those words until this shampoo came out, and then only on the TV commercial. If a man ever did say such a thing in seriousness to a woman, she would probably call the police.

There was also a commercial in which a man becomes so infatuated with a woman on the street that he chases her down and gives her flowers. "If a strange man offers you flowers, he's acting on Impulse." Today that would be called stalking, and he'd probably get Maced.

I bought my wife some Rive Gauche perfume in an Yves Saint Laurent store on Madison Avenue once and the clerk deigned to inform me that it was "Mr. Saint Laurent's signature scent." Now I always repeat that interesting nugget to my wife when she wears it. She thinks I'm trying to drive her insane, but I'm just trying to rid my brain of Mr. Saint Laurent.

Then there's the Irish Spring deodorant soap commercials. In it, a woman in a thick, fake Irish brogue declares to her husband, "Manly yes, but I like it, too." For some reason, they showered outside a lot in the Ireland of those commercials.

Nowadays, technology makes it easy to choose what we watch and listen to. We're the boss. We zip through commercials on TiVo, or listen to singles or WBFO podcasts we download onto iPods. The hegemony of channels 2, 4 and 7 has been broken. My children will never have to watch a couple riding white horses in a field of flowers, in soft focus, for Jontue. (The man, by the way, is wearing a cape.) And they'll never have to endure a woman saying, "All my men wear English Leather... or they wear nothing at all."

English Leather. That's my signature scent.

Forged in Buffalo

BARBEQUING HAS BECOME a game of one-upmanship. You can spend thousands of dollars for some stainless steel behemoth with acres of grilling surface and built-in bun warmers. Sorry folks. Our parents had us beat with a grill that went for about 75 bucks in 1959. Because the barbeque they had was made in Buffalo by Buffalo Forge, and it had a one-of-a-kind hand-cranked blower built right into it.

As described to me by an expert, "air would move from the blower as you turned the handle, down a tube, through a venturi, and under the coals, providing a small version of a Bethlehem Steel blast furnace."

So I took out a classified ad in search of one of these classic grills for myself, and found something even better—a Buffalo Forge grill aficionado, Matt Georger. Matt owns the coolest grill in Buffalo, and thus the world. Matt spied the 34-pound object of our admiration on the curb at Meadow Avenue this February and completely refurbished it.

Matt Georger: We got rid of the carbon steel pan which would only last for a few years and replaced it with stainless steel, with a Type 304 stainless with a finish on it so that when it was all said and done we would have a nice, shiny Buffalo Forge grill. We painted it the original colors, sort of a lime or olive green. Kind of matches your lawn on a sunny day.

Jim: The only downside to Matt's upgrade is that, refurbished, it's going to lose a lot of its value on *Antiques Roadshow*, while the untouched original I locate will fund my great-grandchildren's hydrogen-powered Ferraris.

Matt: Buffalo Forge actually had produced the blowers for years and years before they applied it in their charcoal grills. Those blowers were used in high-rise construction for cooking rivets. Then they took it, this blower, and said, well, if we can use this for making small fires on the top of 30- and 40-story buildings, we can certainly use this for starting fires for charcoal grills. They didn't make 'em with the idea that they were going to be a successful product for retail. They actually started making these grills so that they could take them out as sales incentives to some of their industrial accounts. And they would send the salesman out with a Buffalo Forge grill tucked under his arm, let the buyer take that home, and that usually was a deal-clincher.

Jim: Matt told me that the grills started out as a project to keep people employed in their factory after the war, and they were cranked out by the thousands. They stoked the fires of our barbeques and our economy. Today they stoke a lot of happy memories—and for Matt, with his souped-up, stainless steel, frame-off restoration… a lot of medium-rare steaks.

World Gone *MAD*

WHO HAD THE BIGGEST INFLUENCE on me growing up, other than my mom and dad? It might well have been idiots. Or as they were identified on the masthead, "the usual gang of idiots" at *MAD* Magazine. I used to buy my copy for "35 cents cheap." To a 12-year-old, it was astonishing that adults, perhaps the same age as my parents, could have such a wisenheimer attitude. They mocked everything, especially themselves.

I recently unearthed my well-thumbed collection, stuck in a cardboard box for 30 years, and I'm glad to say *MAD* is every bit as funny as I remembered.

There was Dave Berg's *The Lighter Side of...* strip. Mort Drucker and Dick DeBartolo's movie parodies. Don Martin's insanity. Jack Davis's illustrations. *Spy vs. Spy*. Rediscovering them, more delicious than any madeleine Proust ever ate, brought back the unadulterated joy of reading a new issue.

Remember the fold-in back cover by Al Jaffe? Genius. I met him at a National Cartoonists Society meeting a couple years back—my wife is a member—and I embarrassed myself by more or less genuflecting in front of him, gushing my adoration like a 'tween meeting a Jonas Brother. I suspect he gets this all the time from men and women of my vintage. Sergio Aragones was there, too. He looks exactly like he draws himself.

During the Awards Banquet, the *MAD* guys all sat at the same table. You could tell where they were because there was so much laughter.

Every year William Gaines, the portly, bearded publisher of the magazine, often parodied mercilessly by his staff, took the entire gang on a trip for two weeks to some exotic locale like Paris, Rome or Hong

Kong. Can you imagine sitting around that dinner table? Today it would be a reality TV show.

MAD's influence is everywhere. Watch any episode of *The Simpsons* or *The Daily Show* and witness their ironic, questioning take on the world. *MAD*'s effect on David Letterman is so profound, he increasingly resembles Alfred E. Newman.

My collection is too beat-up to be worth more than the birdcage lining the magazine billed itself as appropriate for. But *MAD*'s value to me, and millions of other former 12-year-olds, is incalculable.

Thank you, Mom, for not throwing them out.

My moose-hunting buddy and Wasilla, Alaska resident Marc Van Buskirk, circa 1982.

Marc is strong enough to take down a grizzly with his bare hands.

Night of the Grizzly

THE ONLY REASON I agreed to go moose hunting was that there would be five heavily armed Alaskans between me and the grizzly bears.

Grizzlies, my new friend Marc assured me, roamed Alaska's Matanuska Valley as commonly as squirrels back in Snyder, from where I'd moved just weeks before.

Everything I knew about animals I had learned on Mutual of Omaha's *Wild Kingdom*, and I didn't remember Marlin Perkins sending Jim Fowler out to interact with grizzlies. Jim probably would have done it, if Marlin had asked. He was under contract, remember.

"Jim, go fetch me one of those cute little cubs. Don't worry about that momma bear." This would have been a good example to viewers of why they needed a Mutual of Omaha life insurance policy.

Fortunately, I had Marc to teach me about bears, and much more. In fact, Marc's wise advice had, in the few short weeks I'd known him, begun to extend into many other areas of my life. Personal appearance, for example. I'd started to dip Kodiak chew at Marc's suggestion.

It was hard at first—little pieces of my lower gum kept falling off. And I'm not sure it did much for my chances with the ladies, although Marc assured me that Alaskan women found a mouth full of chew attractive. As evidence, I needed only to look at his wife Vikki, who was (and is) remarkably beautiful.

Some might have wondered if Marc was trustworthy, and whether this native Alaskan was having fun at a naïve Easterner's expense. A fellow former Buffalonian, Mark Twain, wrote of such behavior, but I could hardly be called naïve. I had previously traveled as far west as Fredonia.

Eventually, my so-called protectors left me alone at camp and went to hunt without me. Basically, they ditched me, which they probably figured was a better plan than having me, rifle in hand, mistake them for a moose. So I spent the night on an isolated Alaskan ridge, alone but for the many grizzlies I knew to be lurking nearby, waiting for suppertime before they introduced themselves.

The mind plays tricks on a man when he's alone for too long in the wild. In my case, about 10 seconds or so.

I began to think how, thanks to the Kodiak dip habit, I'd be unable to outrun even an elderly bear. How ironic if I died because of a tobacco product named after the creature that killed me. Yeah, they would all have a good laugh about that back in Buffalo at my wake—closed casket, of course.

I did hold out one hope if I encountered a griz. You see, I'd once held one in my arms. It was in second grade at Smallwood Drive School. The Kodiak cub came for a visit from the zoo, and they let me hold it. A beautiful, cuddly, baby bear. A Teddy bear, really. Up on the ridge, I prayed that if a griz did come after me, it would be *that* griz, somehow released back into the wild. Just before his great, gaping maw descended upon my face, he'd stop, remembering the smell of the little city boy who once cradled him so lovingly. Okay, I was grasping at straws! You would have been, too.

After several hours passed and I still hadn't been eaten, I began to reconsider my situation. There in the dark Alaskan night, with a .357 magnum clenched tightly in my hand and a wad of chew under my lip, I realized I wasn't in Snyder anymore. I could yell "Mommy!" as loud as I wanted and she wouldn't be able to hear me. I know. I tried.

The North Star above me blazed as invitingly as the neon sign outside Duff's; the air had the crisp freshness of a menthol cigarette; and I had Marc, Virgil to my Dante, to train me in the curious ways of the North. If I lived, I might even stay awhile.

And if I didn't survive, well, I'd taken out a big Mutual of Omaha policy for my loved ones back in Snyder.

I hadn't watched *Wild Kingdom* all those years without learning something.

Welcome, Canadian Overlords

MANIFEST DESTINY, the 19th-century philosophy that boldly espoused American expansion, shaped our country at one time. It's time for it to shape us once again. Consider Canada. It sits conveniently to our north. Same language, mostly. And appealing in many other ways. Universal healthcare. A secure banking system. Low national debt. Lots of beer. And more oil than they know what to do with. Yes, it's time. Time for Canada to assert *its* manifest destiny and take us over, for our own good. Let's face it. We're a basket case. This whole independence from England thing isn't working out. The Loyalists were right, so let's hand it all back over to them, a little late, with apologies for making a mess of it.

Frankly, they've already started to insinuate themselves down here. Florida has a hockey team, in reality a sleeper cell for an eventual takeover. Half the TV comedy writers in Hollywood are Canadian. (Expect a lot of episodes with key characters taking up curling.) And now we're about to watch the Winter Olympics in Vancouver, a transparent attempt by Canadians to demonstrate their superiority in luge, a final blow to break our national will.

Sure, some changes will take getting used to. Imagine 80,000 Dallas Cowboys fans singing "Oh Canada" in French, with a Texan accent. John Candy on stamps. Low-profile, non-egomaniacal politicians. I mean, can you even name a Canadian prime minister? Okay, Pierre Trudeau, but that's only because Mick Jagger was dating his wife.

Look, having Canada take us over wouldn't be so bad. It would be kind of like moving back in with your parents after blowing your money on wine, women and credit default swaps. A cot in the basement, sure. I understand. Mom's using my old room for a pottery studio. Hey, what do you mean you won't drive me to the mall?

If it makes you feel better, consider the impending Canadian hegemony as a government bailout of sorts. There've been a lot of those lately. Although why the Canadians would want to assume our $9.5 trillion national debt, I'm not sure. Maybe we'd have to arrange a quick bankruptcy first, like GM and Chrysler. Or we could run one of those commercials on the CBC offering government-seized property, only in this case the distressed real estate would be the 50 states and Puerto Rico.

Still, before we gratefully capitulate, let's set one precondition. They get the U.S., lock, stock and Long Island. We get reparations for the damage done to us by Celine Dion.

I'd call it an even swap.

Smokey the Talking Dog and other tales from the land of loganberry

Copyright © 2011 by Jim Nolan. All rights reserved, including the right to reproduce this book, or portions thereof, in any form. No part of this text may be reproduced, transmitted, downloaded, decompiled, reverse engineered, or stored in or introduced into any information storage and retrieval system, in any form or by any means, whether electronic or mechanical, without the express written permission of the author. The scanning, uploading, and distribution of this book via the Internet or via any other means without the permission of the publisher is illegal and punishable by law. Please purchase only authorized electronic editions and do not participate in or encourage electronic piracy of copyrighted materials.

The publisher does not have any control over, and does not assume any responsibility for, author or third–party websites or their content.

Cover Art: Copyright © 1939 by Charlene Smith
Dedication image by Charlene Smith
Niagara River Death Cruise image by James Nolan
Ghosts of Halloweens Past image by James Nolan
The Buffalo Central High Class of 1912 image by Pohle
1970s Teenage Human Shield image by Christa Nolan
Forged in Buffalo image by Matt Georger
Night of the Grizzly image by Jim Nolan
Family photo by Isabel Curry Nolan

Published by Telemachus Press, LLC
http://www.telemachuspress.com

Visit the author's website at http://www.jimnolansblog.com/

ISBN: 978–1–935670–74–2 (eBook)
ISBN: 978–1–935670–75–9 (paperback)

Version 2011.06.30

Printed in the UNITED STATES OF AMERICA
10 9 8 7 6 5 4 3 2 1

Printed by Libri Plureos GmbH in Hamburg, Germany